IMAGES OF ENGLAND

EASTON, EASTVILLE
AND ST JUDE'S

IMAGES OF ENGLAND

EASTON, EASTVILLE AND ST JUDE'S

VERONICA SMITH

TEMPUS

I would like to dedicate this book to the memory of my dear friend, Marlene Holloway, who died on 15 February 2004. Marlene was an avid historian and helped me over the years with photographs for my books. She is greatly missed by her husband Ray, her daughters and grandchildren and also her many friends.

Frontispiece: A young Marlene Wall marries Ray Holloway on 9 January 1960. Ray worked with Marlene's father, who introduced them. The couple went on to have two daughters, Julie and Angela.

First published 2005

Tempus Publishing Limited
The Mill, Brimscombe Port,
Stroud, Gloucestershire, GL5 2QG
www.tempus-publishing.com

British Library Cataloguing in Publication Data.
A catalogue record for this book is available from the British Library.

ISBN 0 7524 3712 7
Typesetting and origination by Tempus Publishing Limited.
Printed in Great Britain.

Contents

	Acknowledgements	6
	Introduction	7
one	Greenbank and Lower Easton	9
two	Around St Mark's Road	31
three	St Gabriel's	53
four	St Jude's	67
five	Newfoundland Street to Warwick Road	85
six	Around Eastville	109

Acknowledgements

I am extremely grateful to friends both old and new, without whose help this book would never have been produced. Thanks to modern technology, I receive many fascinating e-mails and earlier this year I was contacted by Ian Haddrell, who had constructed a website featuring Coombe Road and Greenbank Infants' Schools. It was thanks to Ian (who coincidentally turned out to be the son of an office colleague from my days at Carsons, Bert Haddrell) that I was able to make contact with a large number of ex-pupils and all sorts of interesting stories and photographs began to come my way.

Two dear friends taken from us in the past year are Len Bruno and David Hart, whose photographs appear in this book and whose lives remain in our memory. Thoughts go to Zilma Bruno and Heather Hart, who have both lost their partners.

The following helped me by providing photographs, information and general enthusiasm and I am truly grateful for their patience and assistance: Michael Bidwell, Mollie Bidwell, Bob Bown, Bristol Record Office, Zilma Bruno, Clive Burlton, Jan Capaldi, Marie Coombs, Mary Crespin (*née* Cozens), Geoffrey Culliford, David and Stella Davis, Roger Derry, Colin Downs, George Elen, Pat Elen (*née* Caines), Gus Elen, Derek Elod, Debra Ford (*née* Lewis), Pamela Fursman, Ian Haddrell, Joyce Haddrell (*née* Hale), Margaret and Dave Harris, Heather Hart, Pat Hase (*née* Long), Bob Heath, Peter Hobday, Mike Hooper, Mike Jay, Betty Jones (*née* Cannock), Mollie Lewis (*née* Haynes), David Lloyd, Linda Longman (*née* Evans), Anthea Ogbourne (*née* Rainey), Ken Pine, Joan Pymm, Kathleen Rainey (*née* Newbury), Pamela Ratcliffe (*née* Payne), Sonia Reynolds (*née* Rainey), Diane Robbins (*née* Trump), Ralph Robbins, Pearl Sergeant (*née* Thatcher), Diane Thomas (*née* Jones), Mike Tozer, Richard Wendland.

Introduction

Bob Bown grew up in Battersea Road and has written a poem that encapsulates the ambience of this part of Bristol in the not so distant past. It is difficult not to feel a pang of sadness remembering what has been lost: the houses, the churches, all the little shops and most of all, perhaps, the simple pleasures we once enjoyed:

Funny old road; straight, downward sloping,
with one end closed, high-walled, inviting...
For beyond, an embankment with rail line running,
and oh those marvellous moments of trains quickly passing,
blurred white faces to the windows pressing,
and me down in the street, frantically waving
then turning away, though for some while wondering
where they'd come from and where they were going.

The road itself, steeply cambered, with gutters friendly
accommodating small boys with toy soldiers or marbles rolling
towards drain covers, forbidden, enticing
with their black depths below, intriguing, rich-smelling
reminding of warnings of 'fever' (unheeded).

There were people passing; rag and bone men calling,
their horses with nosebags, patiently waiting,
their dung on the road, fresh, rich brown and steaming.

And in the early evening came ice-cream vans calling
chimes filling the air, new and exciting
to children running, tightly clutching, threepences begged, cup overflowing.

And out by their doors on Sunday mornings
were people watching the Boys' Brigade marching.
Drums rolling, trumpets blowing,
such a sight! The blood set tingling.
The leader of the band, mace twirling,
then tossed in the air as hearts stopped beating, half expecting...
but no – always caught. Were we secretly hoping?

And the boys of the street, together growing,
passing through marble and toy collecting,
discovering football, then neighbours complaining,
'Play down your own end.' And us laughing, ignoring.

Then finally leaving, the lorry transporting,
a council estate, new-built, empty and waiting.
Making new friends, quickly adjusting,
but where was the rail line and Boys' Brigade marching?

Bob Bown

We all looked forward to church socials and outings and even just playing in the streets with our friends, swapping comics and marbles and silly jokes. The pace of life was so much slower that people had time to communicate with their neighbours, family and friends. There wasn't the sense of isolation that so many experience in today's harsher and more hectic world.

However, there are still plenty of thoughtful people around, as I have found out in recent years when I have been dogged by ill health. The local Traders' Association has worked hard to make shopping in St Mark's Road pleasant and safe. As we pass the plaque erected in memory of Kassam Ismail Mojothi we sometimes pause for a moment to remember people like him who risked their lives to fight crime, whilst the plaque on the wall of the Sugar Loaf reminds us of popular Llew (Llewellyn Thorington) whose good humour towards his fellow men made his death at such an early age particulalrly sad.

I have faith that we are on the right road to bringing back some of the kindness and understanding which was the dominant feature of times past and was the substance that bound communities together.

Veronica Smith
July 2005

one

Greenbank and Lower Easton

As a child, walking with my mother up Robertson Road to the dressmaker – who lived, I seem to recall, in Daisy Road – I was aware of the sharp contrast to St Mark's Road, with its bustle and mixture of commercial properties and chaotic hotchpotch of house styles. Here was neatness and order, with well-tended front gardens and frilled net curtains. The shops that did exist were placed carefully on corners and sported awnings and door blinds in the heat of a summer's afternoon. Even the chocolate factory seemed to blend in discreetly, with its quiet hum of machinery and sweet scents wafting on the breeze. Even today I feel an aura of calm settling upon me as I walk along this street.

Even in today's sophisticated age, children still love nothing more than playing in a sandpit. It must have been a special treat for this class from Greenbank Infants' School in 1953. Bob Heath is sitting on the extreme left. Even when playing, little boys were expected to look smart in blazers, shirts and ties. No baseball caps and trainers in those days.

Opposite above: Greenbank Infants' School pupils, lined up for their class photograph in the 1959/60 school year. From left to right, back row: Gary ?, Julian Head, James Huband, Charles Higgins, -?-, Richard Wendland. Third row: -?-, Brenda Exell(?), Paulette ?, Madge ?, Karen Hill, Catherine Chapman, Paula Swanson, -?-, -?-, Denise/Dawn ? Second row: -?-, -?-, Julie ?, -?-, -?-, Sandra(?) Brice. Front row: John Hislop, Philip Stocker, Geoffrey Crane, Nicholas Bruton, Christopher Wilkes, -?-, Martin Hancock. The teacher was Miss Paxton.

Opposite below: A 1961/62 class at Greenbank Infants' School. From left to right, back row: Linda Evans, Catherine Chapman, Simon Hendy, Frederick Sykes, Paul Hook, Karen Hill, Gillian Savage, James Brown. Third row: Elizabeth Gay, Vivienne Jarvis, John Burton, Richard Wendland, John Dix, Paul Rice, Vivien Perrin, Martin Hancock, Norma Barrett. Second row: Robert Kingston, David Cook, Stephen Loud, Paula Swanson, Paul Jenkins, David Lloyd, David Mortimer, Gordon Abraham. Front row: John Hislop, Ricky Howells, Edwin Turner, Sandra Watts, Brenda Exell, Susan Smith. Geoffrey Crane, Sally Shepherd. The back row is flanked by headmistress Miss Fenlon on the left and Miss Webb on the right.

Greenbank Infants' School, 1959/60. From left to right, back row: James Mellor, -?-, Colin Glanville, -?-, -?-, James Ovens, Michael Jay, Ian Haddrell, Paul Carpenter. Third row: Karen Hill(?) Wendy Forse, -?-, -?-, -?-, Mary Smalldridge, -?-,Vivienne Jarvis. Second row: Edwin Turner, Colleen Jackson, John Burton,Yvonne Collins, Gordon Abraham, -?-, David Mortimer, Pamela Scull, James Brown. Front row: Ingrid Lye, Pamela March, -?-, Pamela Bartlett, Patricia Robinson,Vivien Perrin -?-, -?-. The teacher is Miss Peace.

Opposite above: Miss Rose's class at Greenbank Infants' School, 1960/61. From left to right, back row: Geoffrey Culliford, John Morton, Jeremy Monks, Stephen Francis, -?-, Lynn Green. Third row: Richard Wellington, Pamela March, Joan Grant, Debra Lewis, Anita Sharpe, Wendy Forse, Ingrid Lye, Ian Haddrell. Second row: -?-, -?-, Patricia ?, Linda Price, Colleen Jackson, Pamela Scull, -?-. Front row: Michael Jay, Christopher Price, Paul Carpenter, Nigel Read(?), Raymond Peters, Timothy Gibbs, Stephen Northcott.

Opposite below: A summertime picture taken in the playground of Greenbank Infants' School in the 1961/62 academic year. From left to right, back row: Richard Wellington, -?-, Michael Jay, Robin Hodge (?), -?-, Timothy Hawkins, Lynn Green, Ian Haddrell, John Morton. Third row: Jeremy Monks, Patricia ?, Patricia Robinson, Pamela Scull, Joan Grant, Mary Smalldridge, Wendy Forse, Pamela March, Debra Lewis,Yvonne Collins, Timothy Gibbs. Second row: Linda French, Colleen Jackson, Denise/Dawn ?, Christina Rees, -?-, Denise Thompson. Front row: Colin Glanville, Paul Carpenter, Christopher Price, Geoffrey Culliford, Raymond Peters, Stephen Northcott, Charles Stiling. Headmistress Miss Fenlon stands on the left and class teacher Miss Smith on the right.

Above: A family in Tudor Road pose by their Anderson shelter in the late 1940s. Daisy Haynes is holding the little boy. Behind her are her son Peter and daughters Jean, on the right, and fourteen-year-old Cynthia Mollie, who was always known by her second name.

Left: Mollie Haynes, cuddling her pet dog.

Right: Mollie Haynes a few years later, with her fiancé Mervyn Lewis from nearby Gadshill Road.

Below: Mollie and Mervyn on their wedding day. The happy couple are leaving St Anne's church as man and wife. Greenbank Boys' School can be seen in the background.

Above: The couple have repaired to the church hall for the reception. After the dreary war years, newlyweds of this era liked to splash out on on sumptuous wedding cakes.

Left: Debra, Mollie and Mervyn's first baby. She is being held by Mervyn's grandmother, Elizabeth Fishlock. This photograph was taken in the garden of No. 3 Gadshill Road. Debra was the first of five children.

Above: A daintily dressed Debra with brother Clive and grandfather William Haynes in the garden of No. 48 Tudor Road. The Anderson shelter is the same one that Debra's mother Mollie posed beside in the earlier photograph. William Haynes served with the Royal Artillery during the First World War and received a number of medals. He was passionately fond of horses.

Below: A fancy-dress party at the Clay Bottom flats. Debra, as Queen of Hearts, and her brother Clive, dressed as the Knave, carried off the first prize.

Above: Greenbank Infants' School, *c.* 1959. It may have been the autumn term as headmistress Miss Fenlon is sporting a suit and most of the children are wearing sweaters or cardigans. Debra Lewis is third from right in the third row, wearing a large hair ribbon.

Below: George Pine returns from the Second World War to a hero's welcome at his home in Bellevue Road. Family and friends crowd round to greet him. His father, George senior, is proudly wearing the medals he won in the First World War. These houses were pulled down around 1969, together with a portion of Greenbank Avenue, and sheltered accommodation was built on the site.

Above and below: Celebrations for the Coronation of Queen Elizabeth, 6 June 1953. A marquee was erected on a piece of open ground on the corner of Britannia Road and Chelsea Road, which turned out to be a wise precaution as the day was showery and overcast. Among the parents are Betty Spiller (*née* Wickham), Vic and Rose Heath, Mr and Mrs Marsh, Mrs Cousins and Mrs Frape. The children about to tuck into their festive fare are Ern, Bob and Ted Heath, David Steadman, David and Barry Couzens, Alan Marsh and John Holly. Mrs Heath senior is also enjoying the celebrations.

Miss Smith's class, Greenbank Infants' School, 1954. Bob Heath is standing at the back, next to Miss Smith. She lived in Devon Grove and is remembered as being a very fine teacher.

Miss Hunt's class, Greenbank Infants' School, 1953. Bob Heath is fourth from left in the back row. Other pupils include Roderick Weston, Danny Miles, Melvyn Squires, Tony Coleman and Veronica Floyd.

Greenbank Infants' School, May 1952. Bob Heath is second from left in the back row.

A presentation being made, in 1967, to Miss Fenlon, headmistress of Greenbank Infants' School. Councillor Vic Heath looks on, as does teacher Miss Smith, third from right.

The Owen Street Mission Boys' Brigade marches smartly up Church Road, Redfield on 15 May 1983. David Stone is playing the bass drum.

A group of Cubs pose for a photograph in the back garden of No. 1 Lena Avenue before heading off to All Hallows church. From left to right: Ted Heath, Bob Heath, David Steadman, Chris Sweet and Tony Coleman.

Diana Stone plays with her favourite doll in the front garden of her grandparents' house in 1956. Her grandparents were Samuel and Dorothy Stone and they lived at No. 26 Devon Grove.

A view over the gardens of York Road and the backs of the houses in Tudor Road. The long gardens were ideal for those wishing to grow vegetables or keep fowls or, in this case, for a young Ian Haddrell to play on a stepladder.

Ian Haddrell outside No. 53 York Road, c. 1960. It is interesting to see an almost totally car-free vista. These were the days when corner shops abounded. In the distance can be seen Hodson's the grocers.

Ian Haddrell with his magnificent tricycle in the late 1950s.

Above: Ian Haddrell celebrates his ninth birthday with his friends in December 1963. From left to right: Martin Hancock, Geoffrey Culliford, Ian, Jeffrey Loud, Iain and Alan Locke. Ian, Martin and Jeffrey lived in York Road. Geoffrey's parents ran the post office in Co-operation Road. Iain and Alan lived in the Greenbank Hotel, as their grandparents ran the place.

Right: Ian Haddrell may have had high hopes of a professional football career as he put in some practice in his back garden in York Road in 1964. He is wearing his Coombe Road strip.

Bert Haddrell poses on a friend's motorbike in a remarkably traffic-free York Road.

A family gathering in the 1960s. An immaculately turned-out Ian Haddrell stands with his mother Joyce (*née* Hale) and grandmother Annie Hale (*née* Young).

Ian Haddrell plays with his cousins Janet and Linda Kendall in the back garden of No. 53 York Road in the early 1960s. The corrugated shed was a coal house. In those days, the coalman had to walk through the house with the sacks of coal and sheets of newspaper had to be put down to prevent the carpets getting dirty. Mistrustful housewives would position themselves where they could count the sacks to make sure they weren't being cheated! The door on the right was the outside lavatory.

Above: After years performing saucy sketches on the stage at St Mark's church hall, Rose continued her comic career entertaining at OAP clubs in Bristol and the surrounding area until not long before her death. No coach trip was complete without Mrs Heath and her irreverent humour, and her name became synonymous with side-splitting laughter. She was a legend with her afternoons of jokes, sketches and musical interludes.

Left: The inimitable Rose Heath in comedienne mode. She is in her 'charlady' persona with her pianist May Knapp, who was almost blind. May lived in Bellevue Road.

Above: Rose and her friend Mrs Steadman perform their 'Royal' act at a St Mark's garden party. The garden party was held every year in the grounds of the vicarage, which stood on the site now occupied by flats owned by the Churches Housing Association.

Below: Rose officiates at a mock wedding, with Vi Allen of Britannia Road playing the groom. The Revd Stubbs looks on in amusement. The previous vicar, the very shy bachelor Walter Booker, once blushed and turned away when Rose got up on stage and pretended to do a striptease act. That night was a talking point among the Mothers' Union members for years and always led to peals of helpless laughter at the recollection.

The Culliford family ran the post office in Co-operation Road for so many years that it was impossible to imagine the area without them. Sadly, though, the post office closed in 1981 and the building has since been converted to domestic use. This 1908 picture shows Ernest George Culliford, wearing a boater, with his wife Maud Elizabeth, far right. In the middle is Annie Page, Maud's sister. The lads are Ernest and Maud's two children, Harold Charles, born in 1903, and Leonard Ernest, born the year this picture was taken. The family had taken over the business in 1902 at a starting salary of £50 per annum. The business comprised the post office, a grocery and a dairy and included the local milk round. Eventually, Leonard took over the milk round and ran it from Hinton Road. Maud's brother lodged with them and worked for Ernest.

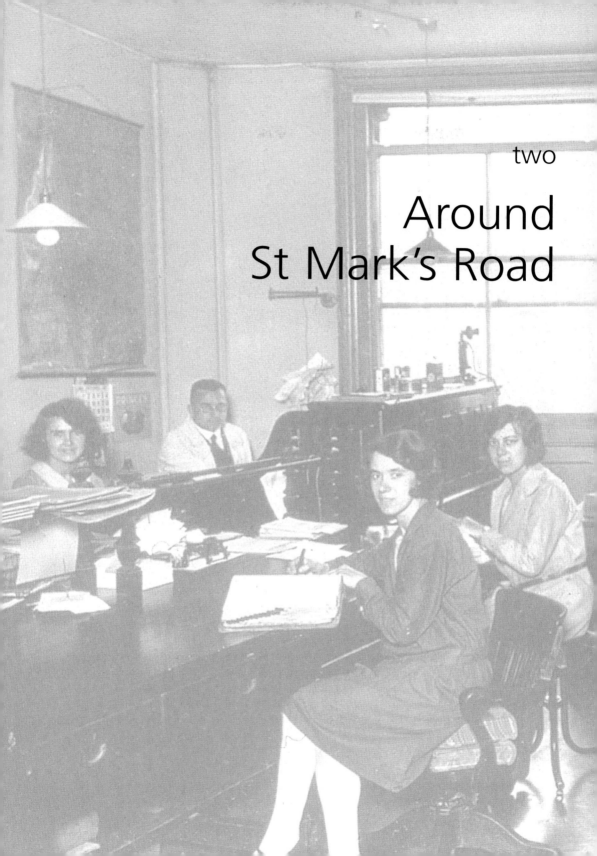

two

Around
St Mark's Road

*I*n this area, there have been subtle changes, the sort that creep up on you until you suddenly realise that all the corner shops have become residential properties. Unfortunately, all these additional homes have brought with them traffic problems, no thought having been given to the fact that most households have at least one car these days. The church has become a drug rehabilitation hostel and the church hall a mosque. We have lost both garages – one closed because the owner retired, the other was burnt to the ground one night, causing part of the street to be evacuated.

Young members of Kensington Baptist church cross Stapleton Road from Oxford Place to St Mark's Road during a parade in the 1950s. Edbrooke's butchers are still trading on the corner now occupied by a fast-food outlet.

Opposite above: In the pre-supermarket era, there was a shop on almost every corner. Thomas Davies ran this general store, which stood on the junction of Woodborough Street and Northcote Street. The photograph is dated December 1957 and there is a tempting display of chocolates on one of the counters ready for the Christmas rush. It is interesting to note the pre-decimal prices.

Opposite below: This used to be a busy little street: in 1947, there were three general stores, a grocer, a greengrocer, a butcher, a boot repairer, a draper, two tobacconists and a hairdresser. By 1960, only six shops remained and now the new school and nursery school cover the entire area from Normanby Road to the railway arch. This photograph was taken in 1996 by Ralph Robbins, who attended Bannerman Road School in the 1930s. The buildings were demolished in 2005.

Easton Boys' School
Bristol

REPORT *for* *Autumn* Term ending *Oct. 30th* 193*0*

Name *Ralph Robbins*   Class *Form 1*   Age *10*

Number in Class *45*   Position in Class *1*

Times Absent *2*   Times Late *0*

SUBJECT		MARKS OBTAINED	MARKS POSSIBLE	GENERAL REPORT
ENGLISH –	Reading ...	20	20	*Ralph has*
,,	Study ...	39	60	*worked exceedingly*
,,	Composition	48	60	*well. His work*
,,	Spelling ...	18	20	*gives great*
,,	Grammar ...	39	40	*satisfaction.*
,,	Recitation ...	14	20	
ARITHMETIC –	Mental ...	15	20	*Conduct excellent.*
,,	Mechanical	32	40	
,,	Problems ...	50	50	
HANDWRITING	...	14	20	*Well done!*
HISTORY	...	25	40	*HTM.*
GEOGRAPHY	...	31	40	
SCIENCE	...	40	40	*W. J. Lovell*
ART ...	...	20	40	Class Teacher
GEOMETRY	...	30	30	*Henry T. Morgan*
MUSIC	...	12	20	Head Teacher
HANDWORK	...	15	40	*H. Robbins*
DRILL AND GAMES	...	V. G.		Parent
	TOTALS	471	580	

This Report to be kept at School till the Boy leaves

Ralph Robbins' school report from October 1930. Ralph lived in Chelsea Park and attended Easton Boys' School, which later became known as Bannerman Road School. In later life, he held a senior position in the research laboratories of the company that manufactured Ribena. His glowing report indicated his future success.

Opposite above: The Harris sisters of Chelsea Road, with a friend, in the 1920s. This is a sketch from a photograph by Colin Downs, who came from Battersea Road.

Opposite below: The final days of the old Bannerman Road School building, which was recently replaced by a state-of-the-art, light and airy structure.

Harry Godfrey of No. 13 Foster Street, pictured at work. He died in 1918, aged forty-four, of TB – a disease which claimed many lives in that era.

Lionel Ellery at one of his many exhibitions. He is discussing his second book, *Easton: The Forgotten Hamlet*, which was published in 1986.

Work in progress on the railway line at Stapleton Road station, 1930s. The roof of the Sugar Loaf pub is visible above the metal segment of the wall.

Iles' fruiterers was a well-known name in Stapleton Road. The family had a market garden as well as the shop. Lined up by the lorry are Tom Fisher, Mr Iles and William Sutton.

Stephen and May Hobday in Foster Street after their wedding, April 1938. Lilian Godfrey is standing front left and Emily Hobday is resplendent in a fur stole.

Twelve years later and May and Stephen Hobday are now the proud parents of three boys, Brian, Peter and John. May is holding baby John at his christening; Peter is standing in front of her. Brian is on the left, in front of neighbour Edith Griffiths, John's godmother.

Peter and Brian Hobday playing in the sunshine
in the garden of No. 1 Foster Street in the
late 1940s.

The Hobday boys are growing up. They look
pleased to be posing in their Wolf Cub uniforms
in the mid-1950s.

Above: The Barnes family, pictured in the back garden of their home in Chelsea Park on 18 March 1923. The parents, Henry George and Blanche, are seated in the centre, surrounded by their children. At the back are, from left to right, Stanley, Doris, Arthur, Gladys, Ronald, Henry and Ivy. Flanking their parents are Albert and Violet.

Below: The wedding of Stanley Barnes' daughter Betty and Len Burlton at St Mark's church, 1950s. It is interesting to note the fashions of the era, with the men in double-breasted lounge suits and the women in their calf-length coats and head-hugging hats. The bride is carrying a huge bouquet of red roses interspersed with maidenhair fern.

Above: The Nickless family of Lawrence Avenue during the Second World War. The predominance of uniforms indicates that the clan is doing their best for the war effort.

Right: Daisy Nickless, known as Nickie, looking smart in her Auxiliary Territorial Service uniform.

A busy morning in the offices of the Victoria Flour Company, manufacturers of Feathery Flake. Their head office was at No. 6 Portland Square. The secretary poised at her typewriter is Lily Cannock of St Mark's Road, Easton.

Lily Cannock's mother Annie, who is second from left in this family group, married Henry Cannock, a greengrocer. In between giving birth to five children, she worked in the shop until well over normal retirement age. She lived past the age of ninety.

Henry Cannock with one of his children. He is standing by the window of his shop, which faced on to Lawrence Avenue. On the opposite corner was Eastlake's tobacconists.

Another view of Cannock's greengrocers. The blind on Eastlake's tobacconists can be seen in the background. Henry Cannock is joined here by his son Cliff, who ran the shop in later years.

Bristol Rovers Football Team. 1923-24.

Lily Cannock and Alex Smeaton were married on 20 October 1930. When Alex retired from football, the couple ran a cooked-meat shop two doors up from Cannock's greengrocers.

Opposite above: Cannock's greengrocers in all its glory, with daughter Marjorie in the doorway. English and continental produce is offered at very reasonable prices, as can be seen on the chalked boards. A delivery bike rests against the gas street lamp.

Opposite below: Bristol Rovers football team in the 1923/24 season. One of the players was a Geordie called Alex Smeaton. He met and fell in love with pretty Lily Cannock.

St. MARK

MAY 1950   **EASTON** THREE PENCE

PARISH MAGAZINE

Vicar—The Rev. W. N. BOOKER, B.A.,
St. Mark's Vicarage, St. Mark's Road, Easton.

Churchwardens—
Mr. A. CREED, 28 York Road.   Mr. W. A. GANE, 35 St. Mark's, Road

Organist—Mr. REGINALD GANE, 35 St. Mark's Road.

Miss Shelagh

In the June 1966 magazine, the Parish Notes mentioned that Mr Tucker was back in church for the Feast of the Dedication after his long illness and Mrs Rose Brown, formerly of Britannia Road, was now in Hengrove Ward, No. 100 Fishponds Road (formerly the workhouse). Reverend George Stubbs reminded his flock that 'From time to time I am sure she would be pleased to be invited out, say, of an afternoon and returning about six. I would be only too pleased to bring her and take her back'. Reverend Stubbs also commented on the 'exciting results of our greater mobility' making pilgrimages to the Holy Land a viable possibility. Twenty years on, a pilgrimage was indeed organised but sadly Revd George Stubbs had died by then.

Opposite above: Church magazines provide an interesting record of social history. The St Mark's magazine is typical of those distributed throughout each parish on a monthly basis. Weddings, funerals and baptisms were recorded, as were confirmations.

Opposite below: The advertisements in this parish magazine from 1950 are fascinating. The Mozart School of Music was a terraced house where 'Madame' Lilian Abraham and her daughter, appropriately named Viola, taught music to those who had aspirations to perform at musical evenings, a popular pastime in the days before television. Pegler and Bryant were just one of at least ten butchers in a fairly small radius. Their shop is now a café specialising in Moroccan cuisine.

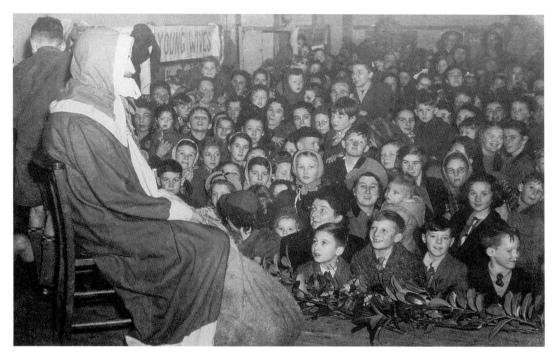

A Christmas Fayre in St Mark's church hall in the early 1950s. Father Christmas sits on the stage while a sea of expectant young faces gaze upwards. Young Ernest Heath of Lena Avenue can be seen above and to the left of Santa's sack.

Opposite above: In the October 1969 issue of the parish magazine, the Parish Notes observed that 'our good West Indian friend, Ricardo Brown of Mivart Street, who was such a reliable altar server' had passed his exams and returned to Barbados. The little boy who 'fell from a tree in the Churchyard last week and had the further misfortune to fall directly on a flat tombstone' had thankfully made a good recovery after fracturing his skull and needing intricate surgery. Reverend Stubbs expressed his hope 'that parents will take suitable action to prevent a recurrence in the future'.

Opposite below: The St Mark's Mothers' Union and the Young Wives have been invited to a garden party in the grounds of St Ambrose church in summer 1950. Among those enjoying the sunshine are Rose Heath, Mrs Steadman, Mrs Holly, Mrs Long, Mrs Marsh, Mrs Jones and Mrs Loud. Betty Wickham, Mrs Brown and Elsie Boulton may also be among the crowd.

Above: Four members of the Easton Home Guard, 1940. Vic Heath, second from right, lived in Lena Avenue and subsequently served as a city councillor for Easton from 1966 to 1969. Home Guard duties included fire-watching and Vic later recalled taking cover in a Lena Avenue doorway when a bomb landed at the junction of the avenue and Britannia Road. He also served on the anti-aircraft batteries and the rocket site at Purdown.

Left: While his wife, Rose, was entertaining the public with her comedy routines, Vic Heath was standing as Labour candidate for the Easton ward. His main areas of interest were welfare and education and in 1966 the party leaflet announced that Labour had opened thirty-four new primary schools in ten years, beating the Citizen Party hands down, as all they managed was three schools in three years.

Polling Day:
Thursday, 12th May, 8 a.m. to 9 p.m.

EASTON WARD

Introducing . . .

VIC HEATH
your
LABOUR CANDIDATE

ST Marks Parish Church Easton.

We invite you to come and enjoy a pleasant afternoon and evening at the

Ye Olde Christmas Fayre

in the Parish Hall on

SATURDAY 25th NOVEMBER

from 3 p.m. to 9 p.m.

Mrs Ivor Watkins (wife of the Bishop of Malmesbury) has
kindly consented to open the Fayre.

Various Stalls: Side Shows: Competitions:
Refreshments: Light Teas: Suppers & Ices
Variety   Items

Father Christmas is expected to arrive at 6 30 p.m.

Secure your Christmas presents here.   Something for everyone.

Admission 3d
Children   2d

Above left: St Mark's church typified the important role that parish activities once played in the lives of local people. In the 1960s, people flocked to the annual Christmas Fayre, enjoyed socials and concerts in the church hall and looked forward to whist drives, beetle drives skittles matches and coach outings.

Above right: Before the Second World War, the Edge family lived in St Nicholas Road. They had a lodger called Mr Philby, who worked as a cinema projectionist. He had quite a crush on the Edges' daughter, Doll.

Below: Doll, however, married a man called Skenfield. She is pictured outside the house in December 1942, showing off her daughter, Persis. The smart pram may have been purchased at Hurwoods in Old Market, who are still trading there today.

The Second World War is over and Mr Skenfield has come home. He is standing with Persis at the top of their road. The lamp-post still has its base painted white – a reminder of the wartime blackout. Naylor's hardware store, on the corner of Nicholas Park, is just visible in the background. It has now been converted to domestic rather than retail use.

The St Mark's Mothers' Union on one of their outings to visit the churches of Somerset. They are accompanied by the vicar, Revd Stubbs. The members include the vicar's mother, as well as Mrs Heath, Mrs Steadman, Mrs Allen, Mrs Long and Mrs Loud. One of the church servers, Bob Heath, has joined the group.

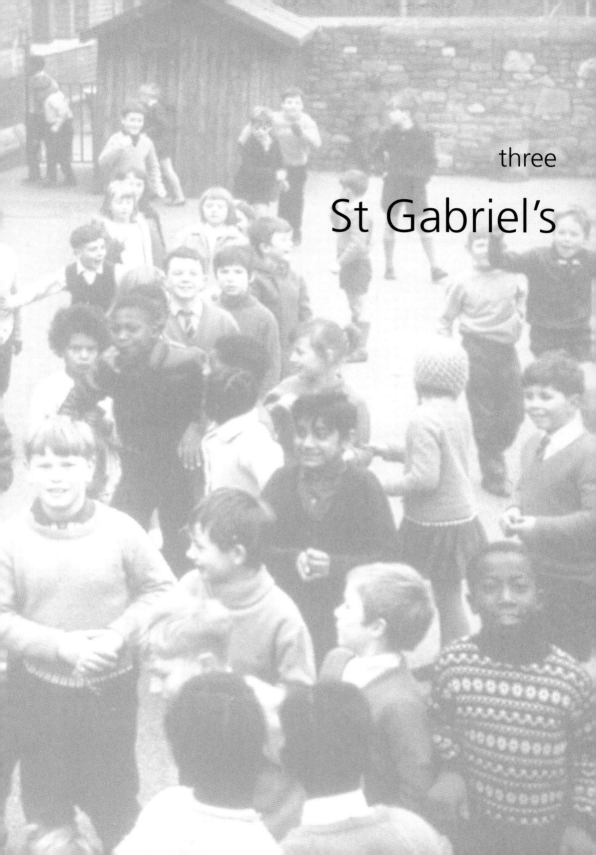

three

St Gabriel's

*T*his area is one which has seen major changes since these photographs were taken. Entire streets of neat little houses and shops were swept away in favour of tower blocks and maisonettes. The residents were scattered far and wide and the area lost its identity and community spirit.

St Gabriel's church, which played a significant part of the lives of many of the residents of the area.

Opposite above: The Sixers of the St Gabriel's Brownie pack, *c.* 1949. From left to right: Jean West, Ann Glass, Pamela Payne and Margaret Southron.

Opposite below: The St Gabriel's Brownies en masse. Among the group are Gloria Thomas, Jean West, Ann Glass, Janet Spring, Mavis Garland, Christine Eddolls, Pamela Payne, Margaret Southron and possibly Janet Tainton.

A Coronation party in Lion Street, June 1953. From right to left, standing: Bert Aubrey, Lil Frost, Squib Harvey, -?-, -?-, -?-, Mrs Eddolls (in a striped apron), Marlene Wheaton (also wearing an apron), Joycie Aubrey, Rose Honey, Edna Dunk, Edie Harvey, May Dunk (standing at the end of the table), Dolly Davies, Evelyn Payne, Vera Thatcher, Edna Quinn (wife of the school caretaker), Mrs Dunk. Seated at the table on the right are Valerie Davies, -?-, Pamela Payne, Denise Davies, Ann Dart, -?-, -?-, -?-, -?-, Bobby Sullivan, Pearl Thatcher, Alan Harvey, Johnnie Eddolls, Jimmy Philips. Colin Dunk, Michael Quinn and Roland Davies are among the group of boys top left. The girls front left are Beryl Payne and Violet Blandford. Twinnell Road crosses the street in the middle distance. The building in the background, where St Gabriel's Road and Bouverie Street met, was then a boot factory and was later used by Schlessinger's jewellers.

Opposite above: Class 1 at St Gabriel's School, 1952. From left to right, back row: -?-, -?-, Roger Brock, -?-, John Perry, Raymond Mills, Rodney Reed, David Mansfield, -?-, Barry Parker, Robert Howell. Middle row: Keith Pepprell, -?-, Robert Horton, Barbara Paine, Sally Watson, Pamela Branton, Hilary White, Janet Spring, Mavis Hogan, Mavis Garland, -?-, Keith Parker, Kenneth Sawyer. Front row: Gloria Neal, Jacqueline Sims, Brenda Sprackman, Mary Jones, Wendy Wilkins, Ann Coley, Pamela Payne, Christine Eddolls, Valerie Braund, Pat Pinnell, Pat Musgrove, Maureen Duffy.

Opposite below: St Gabriel's School House Captains with headmaster Mr Granger. From left to right, back row: Sally Watson, Hilary White, -?-, Robert Horton. Front row: Ann Coley, Pamela Payne, Pamela Branton, John Perry, Kenneth Sawyer, Keith Pepprell.

Class 2 at St Gabriel's School, 1951. From left to right, back row: Rodney Reed, -?-, -?-, John Perry, Roger Brock, -?-, -?-, Barry Parker, -?-, -?-. Third row: Janet Spring, Mavis Garland, Beryl Shortman, Maureen Duffy, Pat Casey, Hilary White, Pamela Branton, Sally Watson, Mavis Hogan, Barbara Paine. Second row: Jacqueline Sims, Ann Coley, Mary Jones, Valerie Braund, Brenda Sprackman, Gloria Neal, Christine Eddolls, Pat Radford, Pat Pinnell, Pamela Payne. Front row: -?-, David Tutton, -?-, Kenneth Sawyer, Keith Pepprell, Raymond Mills, Keith Parker, Robert Howell.

Mrs Hutchison's class at St Gabriel's School on a bright sunny day in the playground in the last decade before the school closed its gates forever. Tony Capaldi from Amberley Street is next to the teacher, wearing a striped sweatshirt.

A class in the 1960s. Miss Marie Coombs, the headmistress, is standing on the left. Mr Colin Webb, the form teacher, is on the right. He later became headmaster at Oldbury Court School. From left to right, back row: Philip Hughes, -?-, Michael Bartlett, Graham Yandell, -?-, George ?, Kevin Cook. Next row: Robert ?, Linda Creech, Lin Exon, -?-, Elaine Mountain, Glenys Llewellin, Susan Sellars, -?-. The girls seated in front include Anne Knight, Wendy Sibley, Janet Wakefield, Diane Trump and Carol Moscokie. Among the boys in the front are Keith Boyce and Nigel Sale, whose parents kept a carpet shop on Stapleton Road.

A class at St Gabriel's School in 1972. The school closed in 1973. The teacher is Mr Mark Williams, who later emigrated to Vancouver to become the principal of a school there.

Mr Field's class at St Gabriel's School in the 1960s. The boy fifth from left in the back row is Malcolm Harris, the son of one of the dinner ladies. He now owns a record shop in Bristol.

Mr Maurice Long's class at St Gabriel's School in the 1960s. Mr Long's son, Richard, is an artist and used to present a painting to the house that gained the most marks in the school year. Richard now exhibits in the Tate Modern and other famous galleries.

Miss Coombs poses with one the classes at St Gabriel's School.

St Gabriel's staff, 1960s. From left to right, standing: Mrs Patrick (secretary), Mr Webb, Mr Field, Miss Dudridge. Seating: Mrs Sims (caretaker's wife), –?–, Miss Coombs (headmistress), Freda Badman.

Above: A typical playground scene at St Gabriel's, with everyone letting off steam after morning lessons.

Below: Mrs Dudridge's class in the 1960s. This was the first class up from the infants' department, where in earlier days the girls were taught the basics of knitting and sewing.

An infants' class at St Gabriel's, not long before the school closed for good. The high windows, through which one could tantalisingly see only the sky, were designed to prevent the children from becoming distracted.

A group of schoolchildren gather in front of what was once someone's home. This photograph was taken in Lion Street.

Two Easton lads look delighted with a Sunlight Soap sign they have salvaged from one of the recently demolished shops, probably in Lion Street. The boy on the left is Tony Burton and the other is one of the Yearsley boys.

Old, familiar buildings rub shoulders with brash newcomers in this scene. The red-brick tower of St Gabriel's church is still a landmark and the old houses in Bouverie Street can still be seen in the gap between Shaw and Abraham Closes, named after former mayors.

This land at the back of Bouverie Street was used as a sports ground for the children of St Gabriel's after grass was laid on what was a waste area. Here, it is being used as a fairground, complete with hurdy gurdy, for a farewell party marking the closure of the school in 1973.

The Prince Albert off-licence was situated where Croydon Street met Leadhouse Road. The design of the building is typical of the Victorian habit of fitting oddly shaped buildings in awkward corners to utilise every available inch of space.

Above: The All Hallows Cub pack, 1957. Bob Heath is standing on the far right and his brother Ted is seated in the second row. Also in the group are David Steadman, Chris Sweet and Tony Coleman. The Akela is Miss Stone, who lived in Chelsea Road.

Below: The All Hallows Cub pack, 1954, displaying the cup awarded to them for their prowess in running. Bob Heath is standing on the extreme left.

An event at All Hallows church to raise funds for the Red Cross, *c.* 1942. The two little girls are Kathleen Haines (left) and her sister Doreen. Their mother, also called Kathleen, looks on proudly from her position second from right.

four
St Jude's

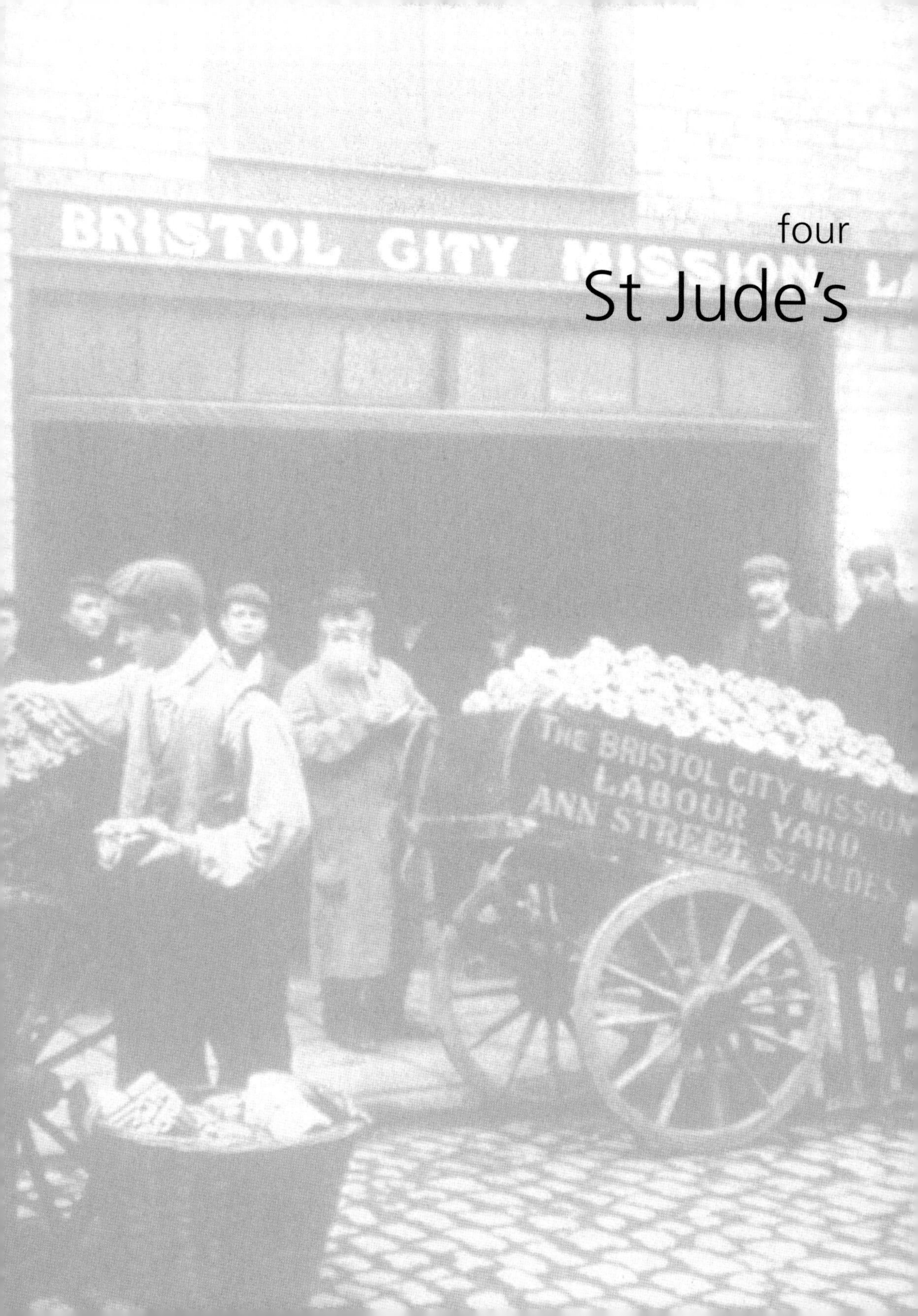

*I*n the past, St Jude's had a reputation similar to that of the East End of London. There used to be a bullring where, later, the church was built and residents were known as bull paunchers. Inhabitants from pre-war days recall the district and its colourful characters with great affection. They remember all the little shops spread out along Wade Street and the dog that sat outside its owner's shop all day and once dashed into the road to rescue a child from being run over. They recall Mrs Manley's cake shop, where people could have their joint cooked on a Sunday, and the paper shop where Mr Hitchens, the owner, hanged himself. They recollect their local sporting heroes, the boxers who trained in Bert Budd's gym – lads like the Pomphrey brothers, who carved a reputation for themselves in the ring. They speak of the narrow cobbled courts where families were crowded into dark, damp houses and of Tommy-on-the-wall, who had a nervous tic. They tell of Billy Hemmers, who had a club foot and no nose, and of young Bertie Budd, who was a Mosquito pilot and was killed in Singapore.

This is the philanthropist John Cozens and his wife on their golden wedding anniversary. The conditions of the poor of St Jude's was a subject of deep concern to John Cozens, who looked for ways to improve their situation and give them some self-respect. He was instrumental in setting up the Wade Street Mission to aid their spiritual well-being and he established a soup kitchen for fortify them physically. Then, to give them a sense of purpose, he found work for them in various occupations.

Opposite top: John Cozens was a great believer in providing a good meal to aid concentration and keep up the spirits. These children have gathered outside the mission for some breakfast. *Limelight Views*, a lantern slideshow, is being advertised on a poster behind the crowd.

Opposite middle: The doors have opened and the children are tucking in. John Cozens used to make the porridge and serve up meals.

Opposite bottom: A cart loaded up ready for deliveries at the City Mission Labour Depot in Wade Street. This is where wood was chopped.

Inside the Wade Street depot. Chopped wood was in great demand in the days before central heating.

Waste paper is being transported here. This was another enterprise carried out in the City Mission Labour Depot.

Some larger carts are loaded up at the depot.

Above: Life wasn't all hard work and praying at the Mission. Those with musical talent were taught to play an instrument and a band was formed. This band would regularly march through the streets of St Jude's, led by John Cozens, with children tagging along behind.

Below: Members of the Mission band enjoy a trip to the country. Even in this relaxed atmosphere, the men are dressed very formally.

The Mission itself was always packed to capacity for its services, with hymns sung to the accompaniment of the harmonium.

Below left: Many of the courts and tenements in St Jude's were in a poor state of repair and vastly overcrowded but people there made the best of things.

Below right: One of the residents enjoys the sunshine. This area was one of the first to be condemned when the slum clearances began in the 1930s.

Above: The women of May's Court, off Great George Street, St Jude's in the 1920s. In spite of the limitations imposed by poverty and poor housing, they look cheerful and the children appear to be well fed.

Below: A gathering of residents in the Lawford Street flats around 1930. The flats were built on what was formerly Lawford's Gate prison.

BRICK STREET MISSION

✠✠✠✠✠✠

MOTTO

FOR

1938

✠✠✠✠✠✠

✠✠✠✠✠✠

1879

TO

1938

✠✠✠✠✠✠

"EBENEZER"

"HITHERTO HATH THE LORD HELPED US"

—1 Sam. vii., 12

Some of the children from St Jude's School, Wade Street, *c.* 1930. The area may have been dismissed as a slum but these children look clean, tidy and well cared for.

Opposite above and below: Brick Street Mission. This little card reminds us that the text for 1938 was 'Ebenezer', which translated as 'Hitherto hath the Lord helped us', from the First Book of Samuel. In later years, the building was used by the Hannah More Boys' Club, under the tutelage of Mr Jefferies, known as Jeff.

Overleaf: A 1934 survey giving an indication of the condition of some of the dwellings in the area. Many properties had been in a state of disrepair for years because the landlords knew that the houses had been designated as slums and would eventually be pulled down.

CITY OF BRISTOL.

AREA.. Date...19.4.34.

DETACHED ....
SEMI-DETACHED ....
TERRACE—No. of Houses ....,   Serial No. 267

Inspector. **Mr. C.S.Hodges.**

PREMISES 63, Gt.George Street, St. Judes.
Owner Mrs. Macey, The Plough, Sevier Street, Mina Road.
Agent
Grdl'd.
M'tgee.

Subtenant pays rent to tenant.

	Family.			Rent.	Rooms.	Hsg. Ap.	No. and Date.
Ten Mrs.E.Glen.	m.2	f.1	m.1 f.2	12/6	5		
S-t. Mr.A.Jemnison.	m.1	f.1	m. f.	6/-			
S-t. Mr.G.Stone.	m.1	f.	m. f.	2/6			
S-t.	m.	f.	m. f.				

Occupations   Where employed

Mr. Glen, Organ grinder.
Mr. Jemnison, Unemployed.
Mr. Stone, Old Age Pension.

No. of Rooms 5 & washhouse.	Basement cellar not used.	Ground Floor 2	1st Floor 2	2nd Floor 1	3rd Floor

EXTERNAL.

Roofs Some ridge tiles loose some joints open.

Parapets

Copings

Front Elevation Roughcast cracked.

Gutters, &c No eaves gutters or rainwater pipes to W.C.Eaves gutters at rear rusty scaly rainwater pipes insufficient.Discharging on to yard.
Stacks Rear bricks loose bricks perished joints open.Front.Bricks loose joints open.
Back Elevation Roughcast patched broken bulged loose perished.

Yard Part stone paved part garden.Stones cracked broken loose water stands paved portion 9'3 x 10' Garden 15'3 x 44'6.

W.C. Accdn. Pan & trap small outlet pan foul not flushed seat patched worn decayed walls very rough scaly.Side wall leaning out.Door frame decayed.

Sink Unglazed stone sink over gully on floor of yard. Water Supply Tap over sink.

Food Storage		Cooking Facilities		Washing Facilities Brick boiler in wash house No door to furnace.

Grd. Fl. Level in relation to street 1'3 below.   Width of Street 25'6   Height of Bldg. opposite 30' approx,

INTERNAL.   GROUND FLOOR.

Front Rm. Size W. 9'3 D. 11'9 H. 7'5 Super. Cubic. ‖ Window. W. 6' H. 4'6 Super. ‖ 1'11 2' opens.

Floor Stone broken worn uneven. Gas Cooker. No food cupboard.

Walls Boarded 3' high plaster bulged rough scaly.

Window

Ceiling Sagged cracked very scaly.

Vent Poor door and window adjacent.   ‖ Light

Back Rm. Size W. 10' D. 11'6 H. 7'8 Super. Cubic. ‖ Window. W. 3'2 H. 4' Super.

Floor Boards patched broken decayed wormeaten. No food cupboard.

Walls Plaster cracked bulged broken in places. Hearth badly cracked Cooking oven grate

Window Rough scaly back wall damp.

Ceiling Sagged badly broken patched cracked very scaly.

Vent Poor bad position of door   ‖ Light

PREMISES. **63, Gt.George Street.**

SCULLERY.	Size.	W.	D.	H.	Super. /6/	Cubic. 307 7"	Window.	W.	H.	Super.
Washhouse.		5'6	7'	7'10 mean.	38" 6	307 7"		3'2	2'2	

Floor — Cement badly cracked broken

Walls — Very rough scaly joints open bricks loose in front wall.

Window — Fixed casement sashes and frame very rough.

Ceiling — Open rafters.

Vent — || Light

PASSAGE. Stone floor cracked broken worn uneven wall plaster cracked broke
bulged very rough scaly perished ceiling bulged badly cracked scaly su
~~towards front door.~~

STAIRWAY.	
Walls	Plaster broken near treads.Plaster bulged Cracked scaly loose b
	on partition walls laths exposed.Cracked ken exposing decayed
	very rough scaly.Winding treads and laths.
	nosings cased broken 2nd fl.wormeaten
Stair	badly worn treads loose no handrail Light Dark No light.

1st FLOOR.	Size.	W.	D.	H.	Super.	Cubic.	Window.	W.	H.	Super.
Front Rm.		13'6	8'6	7'2	166 8	1266		3'2	4'2	73
		+8'3	6'3	7'7						

Floor — Boards sagged worn shaky hearth badly cracked broken

Walls — Plaster broken near floor front wall damp paper loose plaster r Scaly.

Window — Sill patched decayed one sash cord broken bottom sash bottom ra
top sash decayed casing partly missing.

Ceiling — Badly bulged patched cracked broken scaly.

Vent — || Light

Back Rm.	Size.	W.	D.	H.	Super.	Cubic.	Window.	W.	H.	Super.
		14'3	11'3	7'9	160	1244 11		3'2	4'3	13

Floor — Boards sagged shaky worn. Gas Cooker. No food cupboard. Hearth
cracked loose.

Walls — Plaster loose behind paper.

Window — One sash cord broken bottom sash.

Ceiling — Badly bulged badly cracked very scaly.

Vent — || Light

2nd Floor	Size.	W.	D.	H.	Super.	Cubic.	Window.	W.	H.	Super.
		12'6	15'	6'10	187 6	1293	F.2'4	4'2		
							S. 9"	1'7		

Floor — Boards worn wormeaten.

Walls — Plaster cracked rough and scaly behind paper.

Window — S.Casement sashes and frames decayed. rail top sash decayed.
F.Sill decayed No sash cords top sash No parting strips.Bottom

Ceiling — Very badly sagged patched.

Vent — || Light

	Size.	W.	D.	H.	Super.	Cubic.	Window.	W.	H.	Super.

Floor

Walls

Window

Ceiling

Vent — || Light

GENERAL CONDITION.	Disrepair
Sanitary No sink damp walls No food storage	
Defects Poor ventilation ground floor.	General

Vermin Class	B.
Other Remarks	Remarks of M.O.H.

The Cinderella Club. These women, who were mostly from Little George Street, were asked to pose by a photographer who was recording scenes in the neighbourhood. It was the photographer who came up with the name, saying, 'You are all so poor, nothing much in your lives, why not call it the Cinderella Club?' Luckily for him it seems they were all too entranced by the idea of a photograph to take offence at his scathing comment. One of the women is Clarice Morrissey (*née* Evans), who recorded her memories for an adult education project in 1988.

Opposite above: Bert Budd's gym in Great Ann Street. The man wearing the cap is Billy Hemmers, the one who had a club foot and no nose.

Opposite below: A trip to Weymouth, 1932. Rose Elen always organised the neighbourhood entertainment. Rose's husband is first left, holding baby Lena, and Rose is behind, wearing a big straw hat. In front of her is her son Gus. Granny Hooper is on the far right and Mary Ann Gilborson is next to young Gus.

Young Jimmy Cooper, aged 14.

Left: Jimmy Cooper, a young boxer who died as a result of an injury in the ring at the age of fourteen. He was a member of a well-known gypsy family. About 500 people assembled outside the Dockland Settlement to say their farewells.

Below: The St Jude's billiards team, with their medals proudly on display, *c.* 1920. They played at the gymnasium in New Street, which was on the opposite side of the road to the Dolphin and on the same side as the Swan. Far right is Ted Bidell and behind him stands the caretaker of the hall. In the centre, standing behind the cups, is Billy Buss, the well-known local fruiterer. Beside the caretaker is 'Hippy' Bennett, with a moustache, and standing next to him is a man called Macarthy.

Above: Rose Elen and her husband join Rose's parents for a glass of beer.

Right: This is the Dolphin public house in New Street, St Jude's, shortly before time was called for the last time in the 1960s. This is now the site of modern flats. Erstwhile residents remember the place well. On a Saturday night, when the mums and dads supped their ales in the downstairs bar, their children were allowed to enjoy themselves in one of the upstairs rooms. The children would play in the street until darkness fell then throw gravel at the windows to attract the attention of their parents, so that they could come inside.

Lena Court marries Ernest Begley at the church of St Nicholas of Tolentine. The bridesmaids with their pretty headdresses and satin shoes are, from left to right, Pearl Bragg, Joyce Hale, Olive Begley and Phyllis Begley.

A group from St Clement's church perform in a show, *c.* 1932. The girl kneeling front left is Ruth Masters, while Joan Masters is the tall girl standing in the centre, with a fringe and a frilly dress. Hilda Bragg is dressed as a golliwog, which would be politically incorrect in this day and age. Joyce Hale is kneeling at the front, on the bunny's left, wearing a waistcoat and white lacy skirt.

Above left: St Clement's church, which was destroyed in an air raid on Bristol in 1940.

Above right: By the 1960s, familiar streets and buildings began to disappear. This is the view across River Street to the remaining houses in Wellington Road. Hill Street and Dale Street have gone but industrial buildings still stand in Tucker Street. Meadow Street, Charlotte Street and the backs of premises in Newfoundland Street are visible in the distance.

A desolate sight: abandoned houses in Wellington Road and an empty warehouse waiting for the bulldozers. Where the road curves, near the tree, stands the Phoenix, which is still there today. On the other corner of Tucker Street was a little shop run by Mrs Pound. A bystander gazes across the barrier at what used to be Hill Street. The bright, modern shops of Broadmead can just be seen beyond the terrace.

The remnants of Hill and Dale Streets, seen from Newfoundland Street. The place has been utilised as a car park for the popular vehicles of that era – Austin A40s, Ford Anglias and Consuls, and Triumph Heralds.

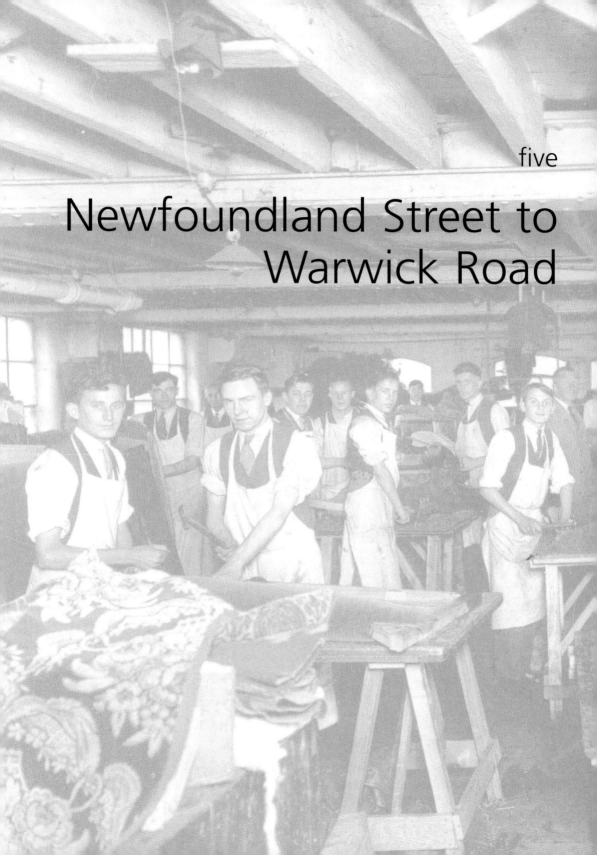

five

Newfoundland Street to Warwick Road

*T*his is another area which has altered drastically over the years. The building of the M32 meant a huge section of Newfoundland Road vanished, and other streets were lost in the construction of new flats and a school. Pennywell Road was totally decimated and now consists mainly of industrial units. Again, a whole community was dispersed and the place is rather soulless today. A large part of Lower Ashley Road was also lost, as was Warwick Road and its side streets. We have gained new health centres, community centres and school playing fields but at the cost of many homes, shops, places of worship and public houses.

The children of Wilson Street enjoy a Coronation party, 1953. On the right, wearing a Tyrolean hat, is Henry Hart, known as Harry. His brother David is near the back, among the ladies with wide straw bonnets. In later years, David worked at the HMSO bookshop in Wine Street, where he always enthusiastically promoted local history books. Sadly he died in February 2005, a few days after celebrating his forty-sixth wedding anniversary with wife Heather, whom he married at St Paul's church in 1959.

Opposite above: Dominating the skyline is the St Paul's church spire, which was called 'the wedding cake' by its critics when it was first opened in 1794, fittingly on St Paul's Day. Situated in Portland Square, the church's parish was carved out of the parish of St James when the area was developed and became the fashionable place to live.

Opposite below: The beautiful altar in St Paul's church, with its magnificent representation of St Paul preaching to the Athenians, created by Edward Bird RA. The church is now used as a training centre for circus performers.

Newfoundland Road Adult School, *c.* 1910. A large percentage of young men were anxious to improve their lot in life by attending night school and learning new skills. It says something for their endeavour, as in almost all cases they would already have worked long hours in their daytime occupation. The school may have been held in one of the buildings belonging to St Agnes' church, as this was where the Children's Mission, the Working Mens' Club, the library and the Girls' Club were held.

Charles Newth and Sons, upholsterers, at Nos 72-74 Milk Street, 1932. The company moved to Kingswood soon afterwards. Henry 'Micky' Cook, on the far left, started up his own company in Wells Road, Knowle, in partnership with Les Burlton.

A class of boys at St Barnabas School in the 1930s. Raymond Jones is third from left in the second row.

A 1959 class at St Barnabas School. Raymond Jones' daughter Diane is sitting second from left in the second row. Ivy Greenstreet is also among the pupils.

Above: The children of Franklyn Street celebrate the Coronation of Queen Elizabeth, June 1953. Diane Jones is in the centre of the picture, sporting a large white bow in her hair.

Below: Twenty-five years later and the patriotic people of Franklyn Street are celebrating another royal event, the Queen's Silver Jubilee.

Above: Cabot School pupils, 1978. Raymond Jones' granddaughter Caroline Thomas is among the children pictured.

Right: This bill, a reminder of life before the NHS, was presented by much-loved physician Dr John Morton Evans, who is still spoken of with affection today.

117 **ASHLEY ROAD**, Tel. No. 56551
CONSULTATIONS—
Mornings 9—10.   *Evenings* 5—7
95 **EFFINGHAM ROAD**, Tel. No. 45295
(By Appointment)
28 **LAWRENCE HILL**, Tel. No. 57588
Mornings 10—11   *Evenings* 7—8

Messrs.

J. Morton Evans
J. Morton Evans, Junr.
and
G. Morton Evans
Physicians and Surgeons.

Mr. Fuseman
235 Glengrove Rd.   *July 1*   1946.
Eastville
                                    £   s.   d.

For Professional Attendance

From April 1 to June 30.   2   8   0

£ 2 . 8 . 0

The wedding of Joyce Hale and Herbert Haddrell at St Agnes' church, 11 September 1948. From left to right: Fred Haddrell, Rene Haddrell, Alice Heales, Arthur Haddrell, Arthur Heales, Peggy Hale, Stanley Hale, Cliff Haddrell, Annie Hale and Ernest Hale. The little girl in the satin frock is Sandra Hale.

Sussex Place before the First World War. At that time, the imposing houses were family residences; today, they are mainly flats and bedsits.

The London Drapery Co., 1900. It was a busy shop, judging by the number of staff employed. Originally, the shop was owned by a Mr Venn but then he took into partnership George Flowers, pictured here with his wife Ada and daughter Florence Ada. George Flowers later owned the shop. The shop is still standing in Ashley Road, next to the Criterion public house, but is now a catering establishment.

Seven Ways Garage, *c.* 1952. The proprietor, Charlie Clapp, leans on a Morris Minor with his staff, Bill Roach, Fred ?, Ray Maynard and Bryan Cowley. The old-fashioned petrol pumps are a reminder of life before self-service filling stations. The newsagent's visible behind the garage stood on the corner of Ashley Hill and Sevier Street but disappeared in a road-widening scheme in the 1970s.

The showroom of Seven Ways Garage, which was situated on the corner of Sussex Place and Magdalene Place. The Morris Minor is on display, together with an impressive-looking American car.

Bryan Cowley, Ray Maynard and Fred ?. Bryan and Ray had just finished their National Service in the RAF.

Above: A charabanc outing, *c.* 1920. The couple to the right of the window, beneath the sign saying 'engineers', are Thomas Egerton and his wife Emilie. Mr Egerton was a showman and his family travelled with him to different locations. His youngest child, Mary, known as Mollie, was born in a caravan in Swindon.

Below: The Egerton family eventually settled back in Bristol, in the Ashley Road area. Gladys Emilie, Thomas and Emilie's third child, worked at the Lower Ashley Fruit and Vegetable Stores, which stood in the rank of shops between Gordon Road and Conduit Road.

The Christian Brethren Gospel Hall stood on the corner of Davey Road and St Nicholas Road, which ran between Grosvenor Road and Newfoundland Road. The hall was opened in 1875 and held a congregation of about 600. There were eleven of these gospel halls across the city. The building remained until comparatively recently but has now been demolished to make way for housing.

Newfoundland Road School, Class 1, *c.* 1955. From left to right, back row: Martin Williams, Brian Burrass, -?-, Frank Russell, Bob Norris, Peter Mansfield, Richard Tattersall, Tommy Herniman, Mike Bidwell, John Mainstone, Keith Harris. Middle row: Joe Mathews, Maurice Adams, Stephen Jennings, Christine Allen, Joan Maslen, Jean Lacey, Sheila Horsfall, Robert Tuckfield, Geoffrey Matthews, Jeffery Knaggs. Front row: Gillian Powell, Irene Street, Gwen Thomas, Gillian Abbott, Sylvia Warren, Edna Buss, Eileen Atkins, Irene Bates, Hazel Brown, Pat Taylor, Valerie Walsh, Christine Harvey. The teacher was Mr K.A. Williams.

A class at St Paul's School in Wilson Street in the 1920s. The teacher is Mr Jack Fry and the pupil standing directly in front of him is John Bidwell, the father of Mike Bidwell, who is ninth from left in the back row of the previous picture.

John Bidwell's father, Ted, making deliveries of fresh fish in the Pennywell Road area around 1919. Ted ran his fish business from his home in Canning Street, a cul-de-sac which ran parallel to Peel Street. Industrial buildings now cover the area. Ted is accompanied by a young Bill Cozens, grandson of the famous benefactor John and son of Ebenezer

Ebenezer Cozens, son of the famous benefactor John, and his wife during his year in office as Lord Mayor of Bristol, 1941/42. While he was Lord Mayor, Ebenezer played host to Eleanor Roosevelt, Queen Mary and other important figures. The Cozens family lived at one time in the Lawrence Hill area.

Bill Cozens, grandson of John and son of Ebenezer, followed in his father's footsteps and became Lord Mayor of Bristol in 1959.

Brecknell, Dolman and Rogers, an engineering company, 1950s. An employee appears to be receiving a retirement gift. The presentation is being made by the foreman, Frank Allen. The company's director, Harry Dolman, was also chairman of Bristol City football club and there is a stand at the Ashton Gate ground named after him. He was always keen to promote sport and was a patron of the Bristol Sporting Club together with the the Duke of Beaufort.

Horace Garlick in front of his home at No. 6 Plummer Street, *c.* 1909. This street ran between Pennywell Road and Goodhind Street. It disappeared as part of the new development in the 1970s and was situated between the present-day Hathway Walk and Robinson Drive.

The old gives way to the new. Highett Drive has been built but a segment of Bean Street can still be seen in the background. A house in Goodhind Street, where the street formed a junction with the upper portion of Beaumont Street, is still standing and a portion of Pennywell Road can also be glimpsed.

Opposite above: Webb Street, which led from Goodhind Street to Stapleton Road, at a time when massive changes were occurring in the vicinity. Some interesting cars of that era are parked on wasteland created by buildings lost in the Blitz.

Opposite below: The grandiose plan for Webb Street devised by Bristol's Planning Department included creating a play area on one corner. In the event, the scheme never came to fruition and many years later some town houses sprang up on the site of the proposed park. The space on the other corner is now a wilderness of weeds enclosed in a mesh fence.

Mrs Sarah Ann Hale (*née* Curnock) at the doorway of her home, No. 26 Russell Street, *c.* 1930. Russell Street was a continuation of Goodhind Street and led into Claremont Street. It disappeared in the 1960s, when Easton Way was built.

Opposite above: Wesley Chapel in the 1920s, decorated for the Sunday school's anniversary, a tradition which continued throughout its existence. Later, the beautiful gas lamps were replaced by electricity.

Opposite below: The last wedding to be celebrated at Wesley Chapel. The happy couple are Maureen Garlick and Maurice Bossom, who were married on 3 August 1968. The large Whitehorn Motors building can be seen in the background. The building next door was once a baker's shop, which coincidentally was run at one time by Maureen's aunt, Jane Down. By this stage, it had been incorporated into the garage as offices. All these buildings vanished at the same time as the chapel. Maureen is the daughter of Horace Garlick, who was pictured in Plummer Street in an earlier photograph.

Numbers 100-102 Lower Ashley Road, just prior to demolition. This was the last building in that segment of the road to be demolished, as the owner refused to move out.

Opposite above and below: The last days of No. 117 Lower Ashley Road, in its last incarnation as a motorcycle dealer's. A handful of derelict shops clustered here for years when all the surrounding houses and businesses had long since been demolished.

Len Bruno is merely pretending to be a milkman; he actually worked for the railways at this time. Soon afterwards, he took a job at Jackson's of Yate, where he spent the rest of his working life. He arrived in this country from Dominica in 1955, the year this picture was taken. Just before setting sail, he met a girl called Zilma, who was placing an order at the wholesaler's where he worked. She told him she was leaving for England soon and it transpired they were travelling on the same ship. Although her destination was London and his Bristol, she was soon persuaded to join him in the West Country. Sadly, Len died in 2004, just one year short of spending fifty years in Bristol. He will always be remembered for his wicked sense of humour.

Right: Violet Peck, holding nephew Michael Ellery, outside No. 26 Seymour Road, where her brother rented a flat, *c.* 1950. The family dog, Peter, is being petted by Violet's mother, Jane Ellery. Stapleton Road has not greatly changed, even though only a segment remains of Claremont Street, the next street leading up from Stapleton Road. Only the houses at the very top of the road have gone, cleared for the building of the Mill House sheltered accommodation.

Below: Warwick Road, 5 December 1967. The top end of Stuart Street can be seen on the right. The houses in Warwick Road are safe for a while longer and Ford's electrical engineers are still trading on the corner of Walpole Street. The Warwick Arms can be seen on the corner of Waverly Street, where Lower Ashley Road begins. A couple of small houses on the opposite side of Warwick Road lingered on into the 1970s. The tobacconist's, in a prime position by the bus stop, was later taken over by Roger's florists

The bulldozers move into Mary Street, November 1972. This little street joined the bottom of Stuart Street and ran into Walpole Street. The whole area was cleared to make way for modern housing, a school playing field and a community centre.

Stuart Street. The hedge in the bottom left-hand corner is same one that appears in the photograph of Mary Street above. This was a compact little community and perfect for children to play safely, away from the traffic on Warwick Road. Every summer evening, there would be groups playing cricket or rounders. The girls were keener on skipping to rhymes such as 'Down in the Valley Where the Green Grass Grows'. Stuart Street was demolished in the 1970s.

six

Around Eastville

*R*emembering Eastville in the past, the aspect that immediately springs to mind is the noise and bustling excitement on a Saturday afternoon when the Rovers were playing at home. There were always huge crowds of supporters striding towards the gates. The other big change is the disappearance of so many shops. Eastville itself, Lower Stapleton Road and the stretch of Fishponds Road to Eastville Park had a vibrancy which has been totally lost. The familiar landmark of the Thirteen Arches gave a distinction to the area, and the sound of steam trains was altogether more appealing than the juddering of traffic speeding down the M32. This chapter recalls those gentler days when church activities and walks in the park filled people's leisure hours and people had time to queue in their local shops and chat to their friends and neighbours.

Ray Warren, the Rovers' captain, contemplates the flooded pitch in January 1951.

Opposite page: Sketches by F.G. Lewin, showing scenes of flooding in March 1889. Flooding was by no means a novelty for the residents of Eastville. Some of the buildings in these pictures have since disappeared, such as the huge red-brick building belonging to a maltster which adjoined the Railway Tavern, now known as the Coach House. The tiny building in the middle distance was a flower shop in its last years, before flood damage in the 1970s forced its demolition. The right-hand side of Stapleton Road, where the spectators are gathered on the slope, would soon be developed as more houses were built along the main road, and Clare Street and Berwick Road came into being. It is possible to see some of the large houses of St Mark's Road, all of which were pulled down for development over the years. The last of these to disappear, in the 1980s, was that used by Ashman's, the removal and building supply company.

The Black Swan
Eastville

The Frome
at Eastville.

Eastville
from the Railway Bridge

Rovers fans in 1958. This was the sort of crowd that flocked to the Rovers ground for every home game, whirling their rattles and with their blue and white scarves very much in evidence.

Opposite above: The Tote Enders are in a mood of anticipation as their team faces Manchester United in the 1956 cup tie. The Bristol Rovers ground doubled as a venue for greyhound racing and the totaliser or tote was situated at one end, displaying the odds on the dogs in each of the six traps. This end was known as the Tote End and the fans who watched the match from here were called Tote Enders. The mascot seen wielding his rattle here is suitably dressed for a team whose nickname was The Pirates. The team's theme song was 'Goodnight Irene'.

Opposite below: Jesse Whatley, a popular goalkeeper of the 1920s. This was his testimonial game against Portsmouth in 1925.

Jesse Whatley.
"Benefit Souvenir" 1925.

The St Thomas Cub pack enjoy a camping trip at Priddy in the early 1930s.

Cub leaders Clifford Long and Edna Hill, who fell in love.

Right: Clifford and Edna married at Stapleton church on 19 September 1935. The bridesmaids were, from left to right, Kathleen Home (later Reakes), Marjorie Long (later Puddy) and Kathleen Hill (later Johnson). The best man was Ernest Long.

Below: The children of Charles Street celebrate the Silver Jubilee of King George V and Queen Mary. They are holding up the threepenny bits they were awarded in honour of the occasion. Among the children is Ken Pine, together with his friends Ken Coles, Brian Thomas, Ray Warren and Gordon James. Ken's brothers Ron and Bill are also in the picture; Bill and Ken are in the front row on the right-hand side, and Ron is standing at the back directly above Bill. Charles Street, which ran from Bellevue Road parallel to Greenbank Road, was later renamed and became an extension of Greenbank Avenue, but now only a vestige of that part of the road still remains.

A group from St Thomas' church enjoying a day out at Longleat on Whit Tuesday 1934. From left to right, front row: Marjorie Long, M.M. Long, D. Archibald, J. Long, Eleanor ?, R. Hooper, Kathleen Newbury, M. Hooper, L. Morgan, L. Winser, G. Hooper. Second row: Mrs Long, G. Greenslade, Mrs Archibald, Mr Long, M. Musty, E. Baker. Back row: R. Eddolls, B. Garrett, J. Wilcox, M. Gadd, R. Baker, Mrs Gadd, -?-, -?-.

Anthea Rainey plays in the garden with her friends on a sunny afternoon. The boy in front is Michael Ellery.

Kathleen Newbury, seventh from left in the front row in the top photograph, marries Tom Rainey at St Thomas' church in 1940. The bride wore pink, with dark brown accessories.

This is thought to be a VE Day party held in the playground of Coombe Road School.

Coombe Road School, 1950s. Sonia Rainey, the daughter of Kathleen and Tom Rainey, is the second girl on the left three rows back.

A nativity play staged by Coombe Road juniors in the school hall. Roger Derry is among the cast. The stage was constructed by pushing together all the tables at one end of the hall and the backdrop was painted by Mr Constance, Class 3's teacher.

Coombe Road School, 1962/63. These children are first-year pupils, under the charge of Miss Roberts and Miss Mallalieu. From left to right, back row: James Huband, Iain Locke, Timothy Gibbs, Ian Haddrell, Jeremy Monks, Michael Jay, Geoffrey Culliford, Nigel Read, Stephen Northcott, David Lloyd, Geoffrey Crane. Third row: Richard Wendland, Richard Wellington, Karen Hill, Catherine Chapman, Wendy Forse, Mary Smalldridge, Vivienne Aldridge, Pamela Bartlett, Debra Lewis, Joan Grant, Timothy Hawkins, John Morton. Second row: Carol Kelly, Linda Langdon, Colleen Jackson, Elizabeth Gay, Pamela Scull, Pamela March, Yvonne Collins, Tina Rees. Front row: Gerald Holcombe, Charles Stiling, Paul Griffee, Raymond Peters, Martin Hancock, Robert Kingston, Lynn Green.

Mr Rosewarne's third-year class, Coombe Road School. From left to right, back row: Geoffrey Crane, David Lloyd, Stephen Northcott, Nigel Read, Richard Wellington, Jeremy Monks, Richard Wendland, Robert Kingston, Gerald Savage, Geoffrey Culliford, Raymond Peters. Third row: Tony Bartlett, Timothy Hawkins, Simon Hendy, Vivienne Jarvis, Catherine Chapman, Pamela March, Colleen Jackson, Ian Haddrell, Iain Locke, Lynn Green. Second row: Carol Kelly, Kerry Hookham, Susan Smith, Elizabeth Gay, Yvonne Collins, -?-, Pamela Bartlett, Debra Lewis, Tina Rees, Linda French, Pamela Scull. Front row: Charles Stiling, John Morton, Stephen Wheeler, Michael Jay, Martin Hancock, Gerald Holcombe, Paul Griffee, Gordon Abraham.

Mr Barrell's third-year class, Coombe Road School. From left to right, back row: –?–, –?–, –?–, Granville Wilson, Peter Parks, Robin Hodge, –?–, Paul Hook, James Ovens, Paul Rice, Colin Glanville, John Burton, Ricky Howells. Third row: Vivien Perrin, Norma Barratt, Linda Evans, Mary Smalldridge, Linda Griffiths, Patricia Robinson, Paula Swanson. Second row: Dawn ?, Sandra Watts, Linda Langdon, Denise Thompson, –?–, James Brown, Christopher Price, Paul Carpenter, David Mortimer, David Cook. Front row: James Mellor, –?–, Stephen Loud, Edwin Turner, David Stokes.

Class 7, Coombe Road School, 1954/55. The teacher is Miss Dawes. Roger Derry is among the pupils.

A Christmas party for the wives and children of the staff of Brecknell, Dolman and Rogers in the early 1950s.

Above: June Gough and Brenda Ayres in the back garden of No. 237 Glenfrome Road, *c.* 1937. The girls are dressed in their Sunday best as they are about to leave for Sunday school at St Thomas' church, Fishponds Road.

Opposite above: Anthea Rainey and friends practise for a dancing display.

Opposite below: A concert party during the dark days of the Second World War. These girls, trained by Sylvia Fowler of Glen Park, were a popular feature at these events. The girl on the left is Muriel Parker, who lived at the Eastville Park end of Fishponds Road. In the centre is Brenda Ayres, with June Gough beside her. These two girls lived next door to each other at Nos 237 and 239 Glenfrome Road respectively.

The new school in Glenfrome Road was revolutionary in its day, with its huge windows, grassy play area and inside lavatories. This was an entirely new concept in the 1950s. Anthea Rainey, on the left, seems to be learning the finer arts of shopping

This was the Coronation party held in the grounds of the gasworks manager's house for the children of Ingmire Road and a section of Muller Road. The mums in the back row are, from left to right, Mrs Williams, Mrs Rainey, Mrs Pane, Mrs Peck, Mrs Chaffe, Mrs Bryant, -?-, Lady Janet Shipton, Mrs Griffiths, -?-, Mrs Ross. The children are Colin ?, Veronica Smith, Sonia Rainey, Anthea Rainey, Ann Ross, Jean Bryant, Susie Shipton (standing, wearing a rosette), Anthony Pane, John Chaffe(?), Peter Ross, David Griffiths (standing, wearing an eyepatch), David Bryant, -?-, Mary Chaffe, ? Bryant, -?-, Lennie Williams, -?-, Anna Shipton, -?-, Janet Williams.

An aerial photograph taken in 1926, showing the gasworks which adjoined the Rovers ground. The gabled house in the bottom right-hand corner was occupied by the manager of the gasworks. In 1953, the extensive grounds were used for the Ingmire Road Coronation party. The occupant at that time was a Mr Louis Ross. There was a tennis court behind the house and Mrs Ross used to hold a tennis club there one afternoon a week for local ladies. The land to the right of the railway line was developed in the 1930s to form Ingmire Road, Bridge Street, Rousham Road and Dormer Road. Glenfrome Road was still known as Wee Lane at the time the photograph was taken; there were few buildings there then. At the St Werburgh's end, before the first railway bridge, were three shops on one side of St Werburgh's Park: a boot repairer, a fried-fish shop and a grocer. On the opposite corner were two houses and a haulier's business. The large white building between the bridge and Narroways Road was the premises of George Hedges, a haulier contractor. After Narroways Road, the thoroughfare became Upper Wee Lane. Here there was a shop and two houses before the next bridge and another five leading up to the Muller Road junction. After that, it was open land until the Bridge farm was reached at the Bell Hill end of the lane.

Above: A class at the new school pose for a class photograph. Anthea Rainey is standing one row down from the back, wearing a white blouse, cardigan and spotted skirt. Susan Ellery is seated third from right, wearing a sleeveless frock.

Left: Sonia Rainey with Grandad Newbury in the garden of her house in Muller Road. The garden was always well stocked with all manner of vegetables, and scarlet geraniums grew in pots in the glass porch leading to the back door.